For Pepper & Colin.

First published 1990 by
Walker Books Ltd
87 Vauxhall Walk
London SE11 5HJ

© 1990 Marcia Williams

First printed 1990
Printed and bound in
Italy by L.E.G.O., Vicenza

British Library Cataloguing in Publication Data
Williams, Marcia
Joseph and his magnificent coat of many colours.
1. Bible stories, English — O.T.
I. Title
221.9'505   BS551.2
ISBN 0-7445-0430-9

JOSEPH
and his
MAGNIFICENT COAT
OF MANY COLOURS

Written and illustrated by
Marcia Williams

WALKER BOOKS
LONDON

There once lived, in the land of Canaan,

a farmer called Jacob.

Jacob had twelve fine sons,

but the one he loved best was Joseph.

HAPPY 17th BIRTHDAY

Jacob gave Joseph a magnificent coat of many colours,

In Joseph's first dream,

he and his brothers were binding corn.

In this dream, Joseph's sheaf rose and stood upright

and his brothers' sheaves bowed down before it.

In Joseph's second dream

the sun, the moon and eleven stars

bowed down before him as though he were king.

Joseph's father believed the dreams meant

We must not forget these dreams.

that Joseph would become a great ruler.

The brothers saw Joseph approaching.

"Let's kill the dreamer," they said to each other.

"We can pretend that a ferocious animal ate him.

Then our father will pay us some attention."

But one of the brothers, named Reuben,

persuaded the others not to kill Joseph.

Instead, they stripped off his magnificent coat

and cast him into a pit.

The brothers decided to sell Joseph to the travellers

in exchange for a bag of silver.

Then they dipped Joseph's beautiful coat in blood,

and returned home to their father.

Jacob was heartbroken when he saw the coat.

Believing that Joseph had been killed by wild beasts,

he put on sackcloth and mourned his favourite son.

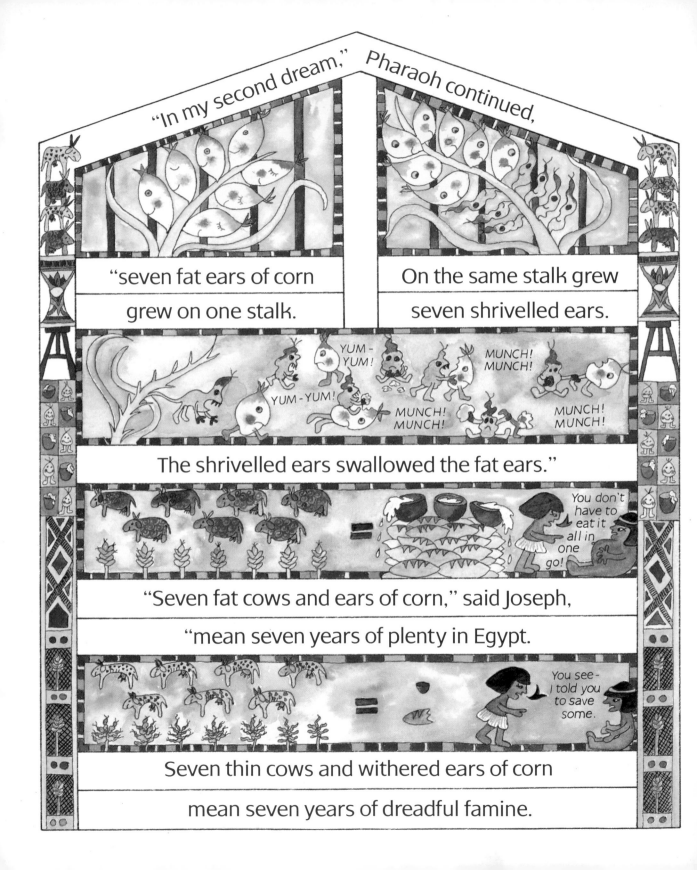

Joseph married and, in due course, had two sons.

He was honoured throughout Egypt.

He had great store-houses built

and collected vast quantities of grain.

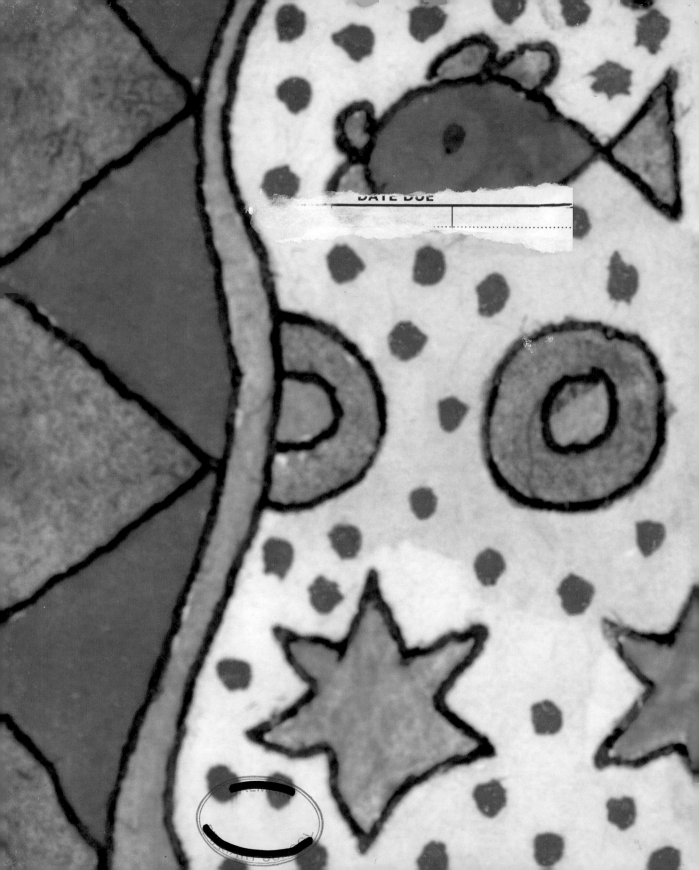